For

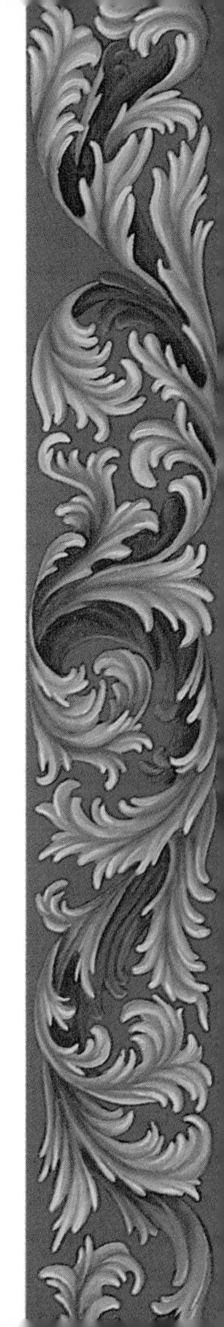

THE SPIRIT *of* *Christmas*

Compiled by Evelyn L. Beilenson

Design by Deborah Michel

Illustrations by Grace De Vito
Wood engravings by Boyd Hanna

PETER PAUPER PRESS, INC.
WHITE PLAINS · NEW YORK

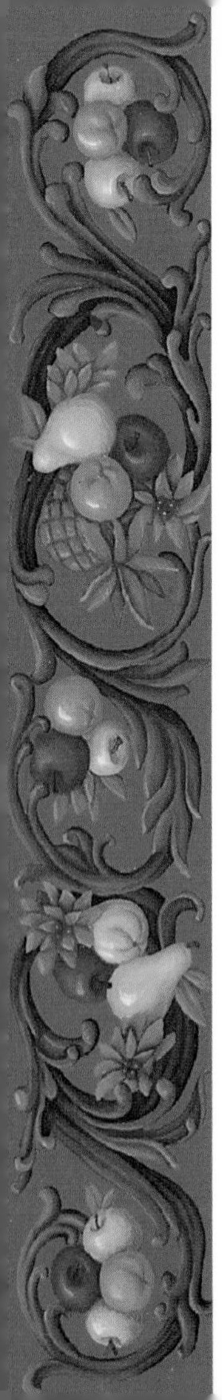

Peter Pauper Press, Inc.
202 Mamaroneck Avenue
White Plains, NY 10601

ISBN 0-88088-855-5
Printed in Singapore
7 6 5 4 3 2

Jacket background illustration by Grace De Vito
Jacket inset illustration from a postcard of a painting by Raphael

Contents

Christmas Prose & Poetry

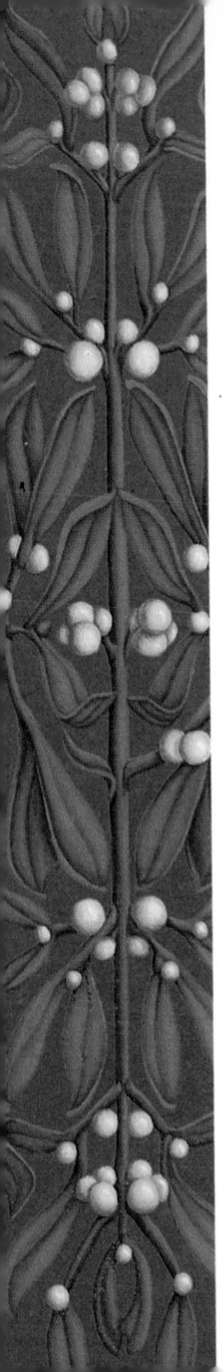

And numerous indeed are the hearts to which Christmas brings a brief season of happiness and enjoyment. How many families whose members have been dispersed and scattered far and wide, in the restless struggle of life, are then reunited, and meet once again in that happy state of companionship and mutual good-will, which is a source of such pure and unalloyed delight, and one so incompatible with the cares and sorrows of the world that the religious belief of the most civilized nations, and the rude traditions of the roughest savages, alike number it among the first days of a future state of existence, provided for the blest and happy! How many old recollections, and how many dormant sympathies, Christmas-time awakens!

We write these words now, many miles distant from the spot at which, year after year, we met in that day, a merry and joyous circle. Many of the hearts that throbbed so gaily then, have ceased to beat; . . . and yet the old house, the room, the merry voices and smiling faces, the jest, the laugh, the most minute and trivial circumstance connected with those happy meetings, crowd upon our mind at each recurrence of the season, as if the last assemblage had been but yesterday. Happy, happy Christmas, that can win us back to the delusions of our childish days, recall to the old man the pleasures of his youth, and transport the traveler back to his own fireside and quiet home!

CHARLES DICKENS

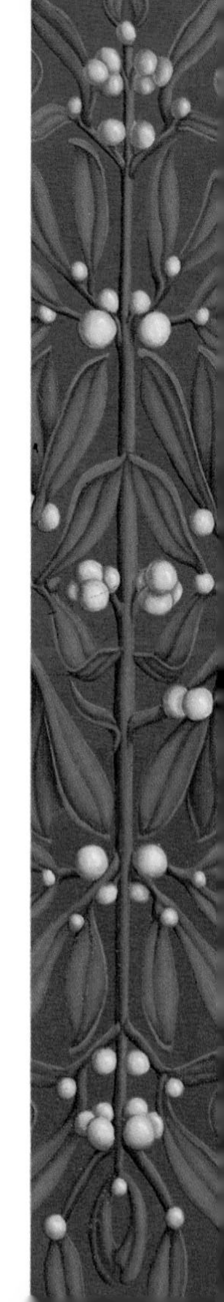

Peace was the first thing the angels sang. Peace is the mark of the sons of God. Peace is the nurse of love. Peace is the mother of unity. Peace is the rest of blessed souls. Peace is the dwelling place of eternity.

LEO THE GREAT

I ask and wish not to appear
More beauteous, rich or gay:
Lord make me wiser every year,
And better every day.

CHARLES LAMB

A heart that can feel for another's woe,
And share his joys with a genial glow;
With sympathies large enough to enfold
All men as brothers, is better than gold.

ABRAM JOSEPH RYAN

You were made for enjoyment, and the world was filled with things which you will enjoy, unless you are too proud to be pleased with them, or too grasping to care for what you can not turn to other account than mere delight.

JOHN RUSKIN

He is the happiest, be he king or peasant, who finds peace in his home.

JOHANN WOLFGANG VON GOETHE

What can I give Him,
Poor as I am?
If I were a shepherd
I would bring Him a lamb—
If I were a Wise Man
I would do my part—
Yet what I can, I give Him,
Give my heart.

CHRISTINA ROSSETTI

He is a wise man who does not grieve for the things which he has not, but rejoices for those which he has.

EPICTETUS

Christmas hath a darkness
Brighter than the blazing noon;
Christmas hath a chilliness
Warmer than the heart of June;
Christmas hath a beauty
Lovelier than the world can show.

CHRISTINA ROSSETTI

Blessed are the joymakers.

NATHANIEL PARKER WILLIS

Christmas is the most human and kindly of seasons, as fully penetrated and irradiated with the feeling of human brotherhood, which is the essential spirit of Christianity, as the month of June with sunshine and the balmy breath of roses.

GEORGE WILLIAM CURTIS

The greatest blessing is created and enjoyed at the same moment.

EPICURUS

He who receives a benefit with gratitude, repays the first installment on his debt.

SENECA

The wise man will make more opportunities than he finds.

FRANCIS BACON

It is one of the most beautiful compensations of this life that no man can sincerely try to help another without helping himself.

RALPH WALDO EMERSON

Laughter is the joyous universal evergreen of life.

ABRAHAM LINCOLN

At Christmas play, and make good cheer,
For Christmas comes but once a year.

THOMAS TUSSER

To a young heart everything is fun.

CHARLES DICKENS

The very society of joy redoubles it; so that, while it lights upon my friend it rebounds upon myself, and the brighter his candle burns the more easily will it light mine.

ROBERT SOUTH

There is something in the very season of the year that gives a charm to the festivity of Christmas. At other times we derive a great portion of our pleasures from the mere beauties of nature. Our feelings sally forth and dissipate themselves over the sunny landscape, and we "live abroad and everywhere." The song of the bird, the murmur of the stream, the breathing fragrance of spring, the soft voluptuousness of summer, the golden pomp of autumn, earth with its mantle of refreshing green, and heaven with its deep delicious blue and its cloudy magnificence—all fill us with mute but exquisite delight, and we revel in the luxury of mere sensation. But in the depth of winter, when nature lies despoiled of every charm and wrapped in her shroud of sheeted snow, we turn for gratifications to moral sources.

The dreariness and desolation of the landscape, the short and gloomy days and darksome nights, while they circumscribe our wanderings, shut in our feelings also from rambling abroad, and make us more kindly disposed for the pleasure of the social circle. Our thoughts are more concentrated; our friendly sympathies more aroused. We feel more sensibly the charm of each other's society, and are brought more closely together by dependence on each other for enjoyment. Heart calls unto heart; and we draw our pleasures from the deep wells of loving kindness which lie in the quiet recesses of our bosoms, and which, when resorted to, furnish forth the pure element of domestic felicity.

WASHINGTON IRVING,
OLD CHRISTMAS

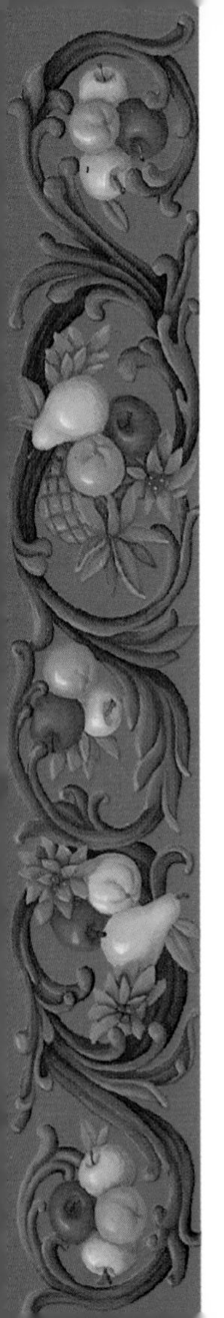

Blessed are the poor in spirit: for theirs is the kingdom of heaven.
Blessed are they that mourn: for they shall be comforted.
Blessed are the meek: for they shall inherit the earth.
Blessed are they which do hunger and thirst after righteousness: for they shall be filled.
Blessed are the merciful: for they shall obtain mercy.
Blessed are the pure in heart: for they shall see God.
Blessed are the peacemakers: for they shall be called the children of God.
Blessed are they which are persecuted for righteousness' sake: for theirs is the kingdom of Heaven.
Blessed are ye, when men shall revile you, and persecute you, and shall say all manner of evil against you falsely, for my sake.
Rejoice, and be exceeding glad: for great is your reward in heaven: for so persecuted they the prophets which were before you.

MATTHEW 5:3-12 (KJV)

To make some nook of God's Creation a little fruitfuller, better, more worthy of God; to make some human hearts a little wiser, manfuller, happier—more blessed, less accursed! It is work for a God.

THOMAS CARLYLE

"What means this glory round our feet,"
The Magi mused, "more bright than morn?"
And voices chanted clear and sweet,
"Today the Prince of Peace is born!"

"What means that star," the Shepherds said,
"That brightens through the rocky glen?"
And angels, answering overhead,
Sang, "Peace on earth, good-will to men!"

JAMES RUSSELL LOWELL

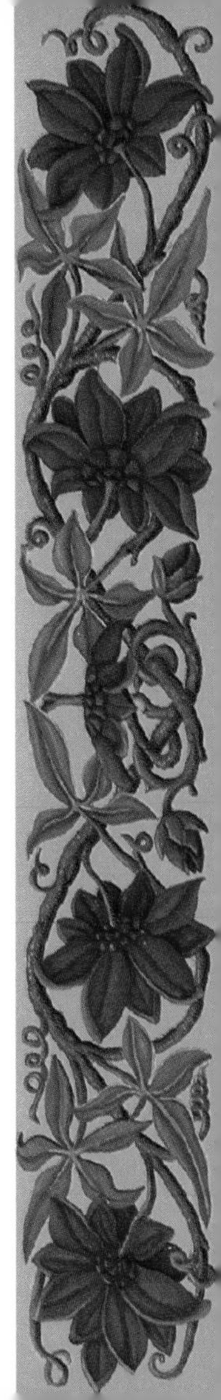

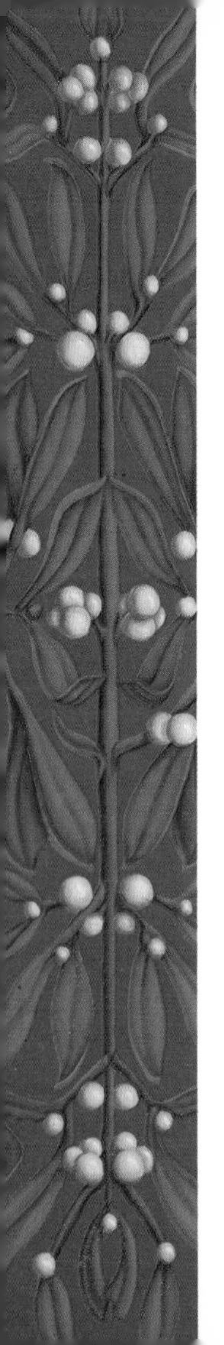

It is more blessed to give than to receive.

ACTS 20:35 (KJV)

It is a fine seasoning for joy to think of those we love.

JEAN BAPTISTE MOLIÈRE

Be not forgetful to entertain strangers, for thereby some have entertained angels unawares.

HEBREWS 13:2 (KJV)

Come, bring with a noise,
My merry, merry boys,
The Christmas log to the firing;
While my good dame, she
Bids ye all be free;
And drink to your hearts' desiring.

ROBERT HERRICK

Heap on more wood!—the wind is chill;
But let it whistle as it will,
We'll keep our Christmas merry still.

SIR WALTER SCOTT

May joy come from God above
To all those who Christmas love.

13TH CENTURY CAROL

The world is so full of a number of things,
I'm sure we should all be as happy as kings.

ROBERT LOUIS STEVENSON

It is in the enjoyment and not in mere possession
that makes for happiness.

MICHEL DE MONTAIGNE

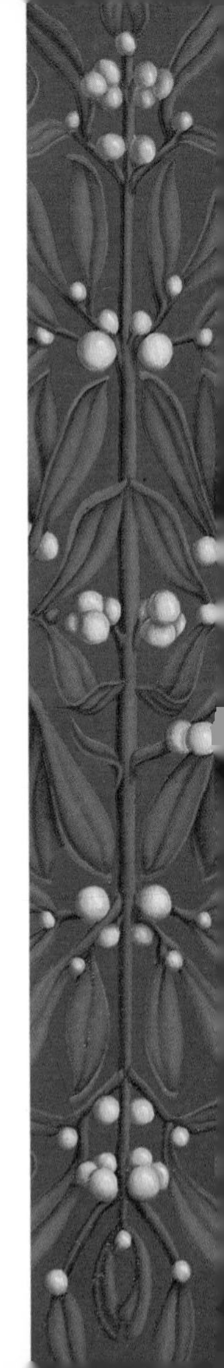

There never was such a goose. Bob said he didn't believe there ever was such a goose cooked. Its tenderness and flavor, size and cheapness, were the themes of universal admiration . . . Then the pudding was out of the copper . . . Oh, a wonderful pudding! Bob Cratchit said, and calmly too, that he regarded it as the greatest success achieved by Mrs. Cratchit since their marriage . . . Then all the Cratchit family drew round the hearth, in what Bob Cratchit called a circle . . . and at Bob Cratchit's elbow stood the family display of glass. Two tumblers, and a custard-cup without a handle.

These held the hot stuff from the jug, however, as well as golden goblets would have done; and Bob served it with beaming looks, while the chestnuts on the fire sputtered and cracked noisily. Then Bob proposed:

"A Merry Christmas to us all my dears. God bless us!"

"God bless us every one!" said Tiny Tim, the last of all.

CHARLES DICKENS,
A CHRISTMAS CAROL

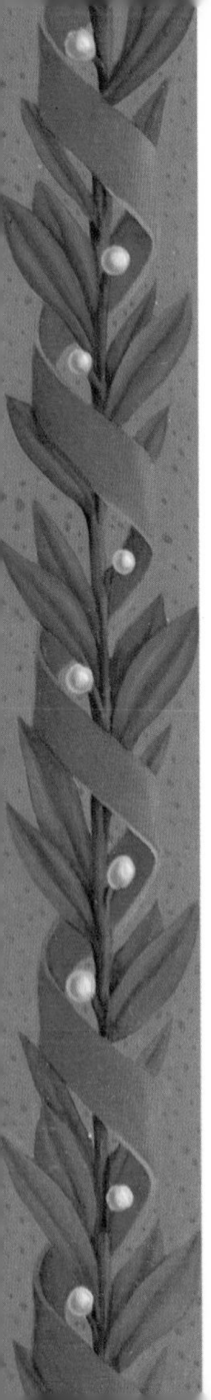

I heard the bells on Christmas Day
Their old, familiar carols play,
And wild and sweet
The words repeat
Of peace on earth, good-will to men!

HENRY WADSWORTH LONGFELLOW

Christmas Carols

We love music for the buried hopes,
the garnered memories,
the tender feelings it can summon
at a touch.

LETITIA ELIZABETH LANDON

The Wassail Song

Here we come a-wassailing among the leaves
so green,
Here we come a-wandering so fair to be seen.

Refrain
Love and joy come to you,
And to you your wassail too,
And God bless you and send you a happy
New Year.

We are the daily beggars that beg from
door to door,
But we are neighbors' children whom you
have seen before.

Refrain

God bless the master of this house,
likewise the mistress too.
And all the little children around the table go.

Refrain

THE FIRST NOWELL

Nowell, Nowell, Nowell, Nowell,
Born is the King of Israel.

The first Nowell, the angels did say,
Was to certain poor shepherds in fields as
they lay;
In fields where they lay keeping their sheep,
On a cold winter's night that was so deep.

Nowell, Nowell, Nowell, Nowell,
Born is the King of Israel.
Nowell, Nowell, Nowell.

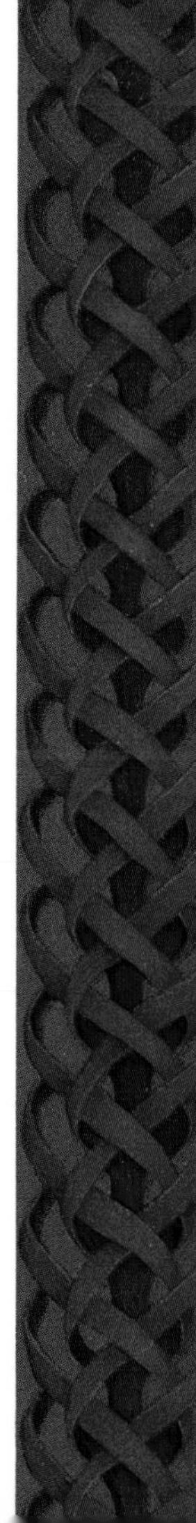

Angels We Have Heard on High

Angels we have heard on high,
Sweetly singing o'er the plains,
And the mountains in reply,
Echoing their joyous strains.
Gloria in excelsis Deo,
Gloria in excelsis Deo.

Shepherds, why this jubilee?
Why your joyous songs prolong?
What the gladsome tidings be
Which inspire your heav'nly song?
Gloria in excelsis Deo,
Gloria in excelsis Deo.

Come to Bethlehem and see
Him whose birth the angels sing;
Come, adore on bended knee,
Christ the Lord, the newborn King.
Gloria in excelsis Deo,
Gloria in excelsis Deo.

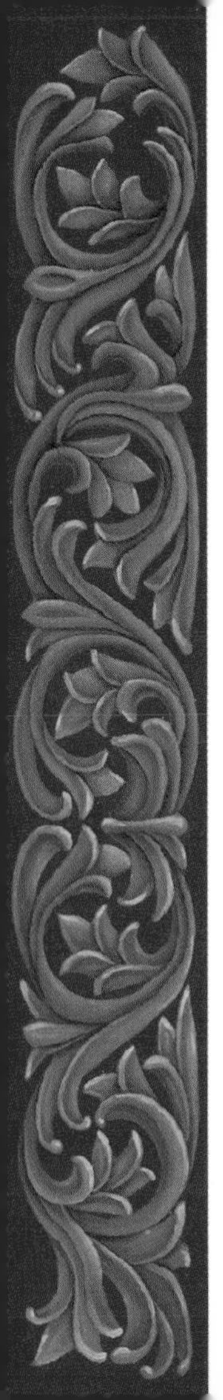

O Little Town of Bethlehem

O little town of Bethlehem,
How still we see thee lie!
Above thy deep and dreamless sleep,
The silent stars go by;
Yet in thy dark streets shineth
The everlasting Light;
The hopes and fears of all the years
Are met in thee tonight.

For Christ is born of Mary,
And gathered all above,
While mortals sleep, the angels keep
Their watch of wond'ring love.
O morning stars, together
Proclaim the holy birth,
And praises sing to God the King,
And peace to men on earth!

O holy Child of Bethlehem,
Descend to us, we pray;

Cast out our sin and enter in;
Be born in us today!
We hear the Christmas Angels
The great glad tidings tell;
O come to us, abide with us
Our Lord Emmanuel!

Away in a Manger

Away in a manger,
No crib nor a bed,
The little Lord Jesus
Laid down His sweet head.
The stars in the sky,
Looked down where He lay,
The little Lord Jesus
Asleep on the hay.

The cattle are lowing,
The poor baby wakes,
But little Lord Jesus
No crying He makes.
I love Thee, Lord Jesus,
Look down from the sky,
And sit by my cradle
Till morning is nigh.

Be near me Lord Jesus
I ask Thee to stay

Close by me forever,
And love me I pray,
Bless all the dear children
In thy tender care
And take us to heaven
To live with Thee there.

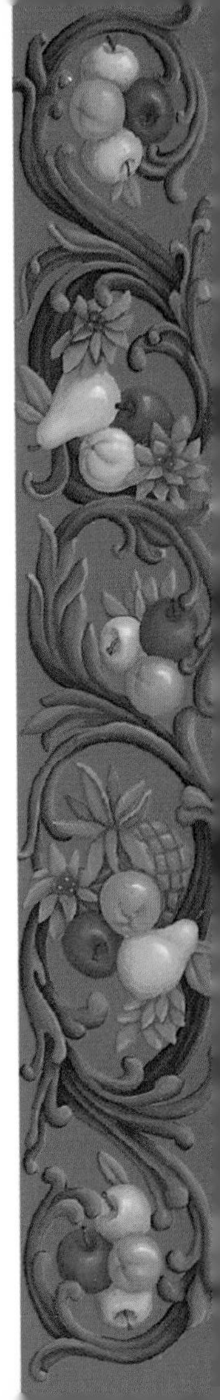

Silent Night

Silent night, holy night!
All is calm, all is bright
Round yon Virgin Mother and Child.
Holy Infant so tender and mild,
Sleep in heavenly peace,
Sleep in heavenly peace.

Silent night, holy night!
Shepherds quake at the sight!
Glories stream from heaven afar,
Heav'nly hosts sing Alleluia;
Christ, the Savior, is born,
Christ, the Savior, is born.

Silent night, holy night!
Son of God, love's pure light
Radiant beams from Thy holy face
With the dawn of redeeming grace,
Jesus, Lord, at Thy birth,
Jesus, Lord, at Thy birth.

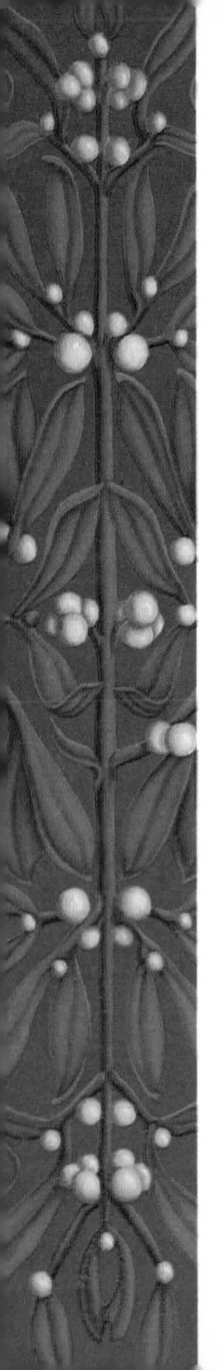

We Wish You a Merry Christmas

Refrain
We wish you a merry Christmas
We wish you a merry Christmas
We wish you a merry Christmas
And a happy New Year.

Good tidings we bring for you and your kin.
We wish you a Merry Christmas and a
happy New Year.

Refrain

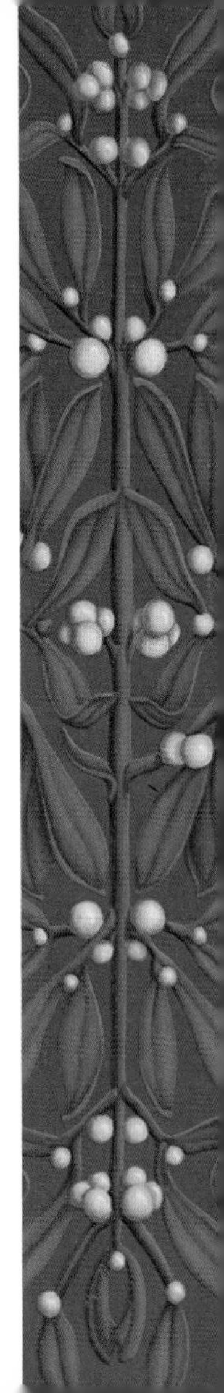

A Tree-Trimming Party Menu

Mulled Cider Punch

Egg Nog

Hot Spiced Cranberry Punch

Egg Nog Pie

Christmas Fruit Cake

English Plum Pudding with Hard Sauce

Mincemeat Pie

Chocolate Mousse

Chocolate Roll

Viennese Yuletide Crescents

Sugar Cookies

Mulled Cider Punch

6 quarts cider
2 teaspoons whole cloves
3 sticks cinnamon
1/2 teaspoon nutmeg
3/4 cup sugar

Combine cider, cloves, cinnamon, nutmeg, and sugar; bring to boil for 5 minutes; strain. Serve hot.

20 to 25 servings

Egg Nog

8 eggs, separated
6 tablespoons sugar
6 cups milk
Rum or rum flavoring to taste
2 cups heavy cream
Nutmeg

Beat egg yolks and sugar together until thick and pale. Stir in milk and rum or rum flavoring. Beat egg whites until stiff. Whip cream. Fold egg whites into egg yolk mixture and fold in whipped cream. Add more sugar if necessary. Pour into punch bowl and sprinkle surface with nutmeg.

10 servings

Hot Spiced Cranberry Punch

3/4 cup firmly packed brown sugar
1/4 teaspoon nutmeg
1/2 teaspoon cinnamon
1/2 teaspoon allspice
3/4 teaspoon cloves
2 16-ounce cans jellied cranberry sauce
1 quart pineapple juice
Butter or margarine
Cinnamon sticks

Bring sugar, 1 cup water, and spices to a boil. Crush cranberry sauce with fork. Add 3 cups water to cranberry sauce and beat with rotary beater until smooth. Add cranberry liquid and pineapple juice to hot spiced syrup and heat to boiling. Serve hot. Dot with butter or margarine. Serve with cinnamon stick stirrers.

2-1/2 quarts

Egg Nog Pie

3 eggs, separated
1/2 cup sugar
2 cups light cream
1/8 teaspoon salt
1/4 teaspoon nutmeg
Rum or rum flavoring to taste
Pastry dough for 9-inch 1-crust pie
Slightly sweetened whipped cream (optional)
Candied rinds to garnish

Beat egg yolks, sugar, and cream. Add salt, nutmeg, and rum or rum flavoring. Beat egg whites until stiff and fold into mixture. Pour into unbaked pie shell. Bake in 450° oven 10 minutes, then at 325° until firm, about 25 minutes. For a very rich dessert, top with slightly sweetened whipped cream. Garnish pie with red and green candy flowers, made from candied rinds.

Christmas Fruit Cake

1/2 pound chopped candied cherries
1/4 pound chopped candied citron
1/4 pound chopped walnuts
1/4 pound chopped pecans
1/2 pound raisins
1/4 pound lemon peel, cut up
1/4 pound orange peel, cut up
1-3/4 cups all-purpose flour, divided
1 cup butter
1/2 cup sugar
1/2 cup honey
5 eggs, beaten
1 teaspoon salt
1 teaspoon baking powder
1 teaspoon allspice
1/2 teaspoon nutmeg
1/2 teaspoon cinnamon
1/2 teaspoon cloves

1/4 cup orange or grape juice
Almonds and cherries to garnish (optional)
Brandy (optional)

Combine candied fruits, nuts, raisins, lemon and orange peel. Dredge in 1/4 cup flour. Cream butter and sugar; add honey, then eggs, and beat well. Sift remaining 1-1/2 cups flour with dry ingredients and add alternately with fruit juice, beating thoroughly. Pour batter over floured fruits and mix well. Line 2 greased 7-1/2 inch x 3-1/2 inch loaf pans with waxed paper, allowing 1/2 inch to extend above all sides of pans. Pour batter into pans; do not flatten. Put another pan holding 2 cups water on bottom shelf of oven. Bake in 250° oven 3 to 4 hours. If decoration of almonds and cherries is used, place on cake at end of 2 hours. If desired, pour brandy over cake and wrap in brandy-soaked cloth. Store in covered container in a cool place.

English Plum Pudding

10 slices white bread
1 cup scalded milk
1/2 cup sugar
4 eggs, separated
1-1/3 cups golden raisins, lightly floured
1/2 cup finely chopped dates
3 tablespoons finely chopped citron
3/4 cup finely chopped suet
3 tablespoons brandy (optional)
1 teaspoon nutmeg
1/2 teaspoon cinnamon
1/4 teaspoon ground cloves
1/4 teaspoon mace
1 teaspoon salt

Crumb bread and soak in hot milk. Cool and add sugar, egg yolks, raisins, dates, and citron. Cream suet in food processor and add to crumb mixture.

Stir in brandy (if desired), nutmeg, cinnamon, cloves, mace, and salt. Beat until well blended. Beat egg whites until stiff but not dry. Stir a third of the egg whites into pudding mixture; gently fold in the remainder. Spoon mixture into a buttered 2-quart mold and cover. Steam for 6 hours in a large covered pot holding boiling water to come halfway up the sides of the mold. Remove and let cool for 10 minutes before unmolding. Serve with warm hard sauce.

Hard Sauce

5 tablespoons butter
1 cup confectioners sugar
1/2 teaspoon vanilla

Cream butter, add sugar, and beat with electric beater until pale and creamy. Add vanilla and blend. Cover and refrigerate until needed.

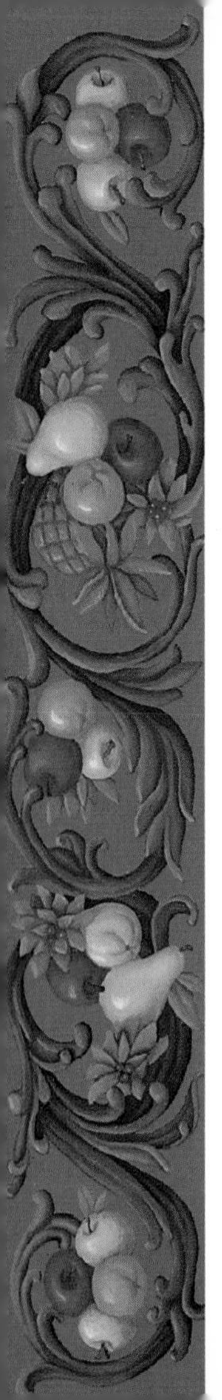

Mincemeat Pie

1 can (1-2/3 cups) mincemeat
2 cups thin-sliced apples
1 teaspoon grated lemon peel
2 tablespoons lemon juice
Pastry dough for 9-inch 2-crust pie

Combine mincemeat, apples, lemon peel, and juice; heat thoroughly. Pour into 9-inch pastry-lined pie pan; adjust top crust. Sprinkle with a small amount of sugar and bake in 400° oven 35 minutes.

Chocolate Mousse

4 ounces semi-sweet chocolate morsels
5 eggs, separated
3 tablespoons sugar
1/2 pint heavy cream
2 tablespoons brandy (optional)

Melt chocolate morsels in top of double boiler. Put into bowl and add beaten egg yolks. Mix thoroughly. In another bowl add sugar to heavy cream and whip. Add whipped cream to chocolate mixture. Beat egg whites until stiff and fold into chocolate mixture. Add brandy, if desired. Pour into serving bowl and refrigerate for at least 10 hours.

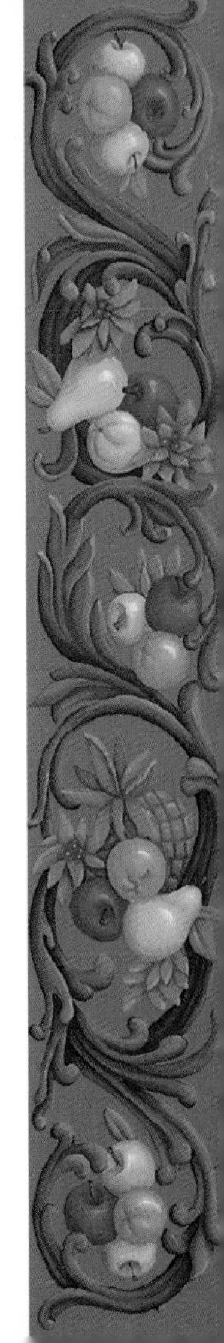

Chocolate Roll

5 large eggs, separated
2/3 cup sugar
6 ounces semi-sweet chocolate
3 tablespoons strong coffee
Cocoa
1-1/4 cups heavy cream, whipped

Butter 8-inch x 12-inch baking sheet. Line with waxed paper and butter paper. Beat egg yolks and sugar with rotary beater or electric mixer until thick and pale in color.

Combine chocolate and coffee and place over low heat in double boiler. Stir until chocolate melts. Let mixture cool slightly and stir into egg yolks. Beat egg whites until stiff and fold in. Spread mixture evenly on prepared baking sheet and bake 14 minutes in 350° oven, or until knife inserted in middle comes out clean. Do not overbake.

Remove pan from oven and cover cake with a damp cloth. Let stand 30 minutes or until cool. Loosen cake from baking sheet and dust cake generously with cocoa. Turn cake out on waxed paper, cocoa side down, and carefully remove paper from bottom of cake. Spread cake with whipped cream, sweetened and flavored to taste, and roll up like a jelly roll. For easy rolling, firmly grasp each corner of waxed paper on which cake was turned out and flip over about two inches of edge on top of cake. Continue to roll by further lifting waxed paper. The last roll should deposit log on a long platter. Cover top with whipped cream. Garnish with chocolate shavings.

8 servings

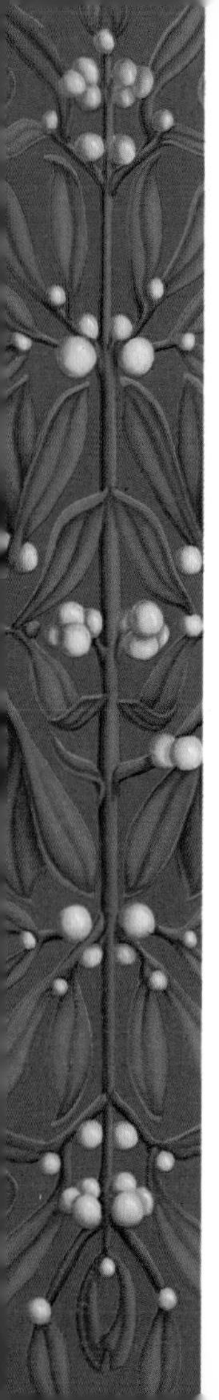

Viennese Yuletide Crescents

1 cup soft butter
1/3 cup granulated sugar
2/3 cup chopped almonds
1/4 teaspoon salt
2 cups all-purpose flour
Confectioners sugar

Mix first 4 ingredients together thoroughly; work in flour with hands. Chill dough. Pull off small pieces of chilled dough and work with hands until pliable but not sticky. Roll between palms into pencil-thick strips and shape into small crescents on ungreased cookie sheets. Bake at 350° until set but not brown (about 15 minutes). Remove from cookie sheets when cooled and roll in confectioners sugar.

75 cookies

Sugar Cookies

1/2 cup soft butter
1/2 cup sugar
1 egg
1 tablespoon milk or cream
1/2 teaspoon vanilla
1/2 teaspoon lemon extract
1-1/2 cups flour
1/2 teaspoon baking soda
1/4 teaspoon salt
Colored sugar

Combine ingredients in above order. Chill dough. Roll out very thin, about 1/16-inch thick. Cut into fancy shapes with cookie cutters; sprinkle with colored sugar and bake at 350° on greased cookie sheets until very lightly browned—about 5-6 minutes. Watch carefully to keep from over-browning.

About 80 small cookies

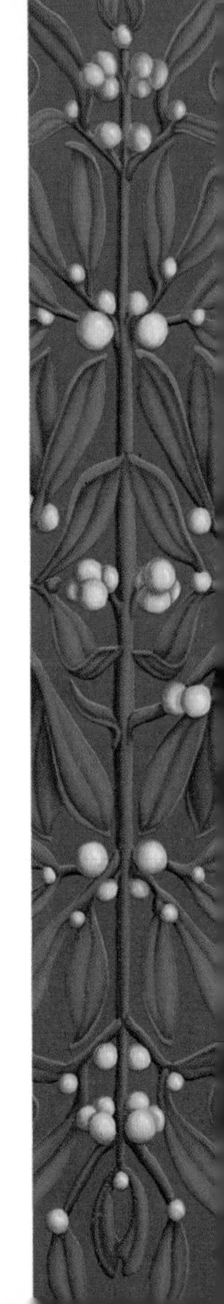